First World War
and Army of Occupation
War Diary
France, Belgium and Germany

31 DIVISION
Divisional Troops
Divisional Ammunition Column
3 April 1916 - 30 April 1919

WO95/2351/1

The Naval & Military Press Ltd
www.nmarchive.com
Published in association with The National Archives

Published by

The Naval & Military Press Ltd
Unit 10 Ridgewood Industrial Park,
Uckfield, East Sussex,
TN22 5QE England
Tel: +44 (0) 1825 749494

www.naval-military-press.com
www.nmarchive.com

This diary has been reprinted in facsimile from the original. Any imperfections are inevitably reproduced and the quality may fall short of modern type and cartographic standards.

© **Crown Copyright**
Images reproduced by permission of The National Archives, London, England, 2015.

Contents

Document type	Place/Title	Date From	Date To
Heading	WO95/2351 Div Amm Column Apr 16-Feb19		
Heading	31st Division Divl Artillery 31st Divl Ammn Col. Apr 1916- Apr 1919		
War Diary	Marseilles	03/04/1916	04/04/1916
War Diary	Abbeville	06/04/1916	06/04/1916
War Diary	Doullens	06/04/1916	06/04/1916
War Diary	Amplier	06/04/1916	06/04/1916
War Diary	Abbeville	07/04/1916	07/04/1916
War Diary	Amplier	08/04/1916	08/04/1916
War Diary	Thievres	11/04/1916	15/05/1916
War Diary	Authie	15/05/1916	15/05/1916
War Diary	Thievres	19/05/1916	31/05/1916
War Diary	Thievres Authie	01/06/1916	08/06/1916
War Diary	Buswood	08/06/1916	08/06/1916
War Diary	Thievres Buswood	08/06/1916	22/06/1916
War Diary	Buswood	22/06/1916	26/06/1916
Heading	31st Division. War Diary Divisional Ammunition Column R.F.A. 1st To 31st July 1916		
Heading	War Diary Of 31st Divn Armm Col. 1st July To 31st July 1916		
War Diary	Bus	01/07/1916	01/07/1916
War Diary	Occoches	06/07/1916	06/07/1916
War Diary	Bus	07/07/1916	07/07/1916
War Diary	Occoches	08/07/1916	08/07/1916
War Diary	Thiennes & Tannay	09/07/1916	10/07/1916
War Diary	Croix Marmuse	15/07/1916	25/07/1916
Heading	Confidential War Diary Of 31st Divl. Ammn. Column. From August 1st 1916 To August 31st 1916 Volume VIII		
War Diary	Croix Marmuse	01/08/1916	31/08/1916
Heading	Confidential War Diary Of 31st Divl. Ammn. Column From 1st September 1916 To 30th September 1916. Volume IX		
War Diary	Croix Marmuse	01/09/1916	18/09/1916
War Diary	Bethune	18/09/1916	30/09/1916
Heading	Confidential War Diary Of 31st Divisional Ammunition Column. From 1st October 1916 To 31st October 1916. Volume X		
War Diary	Bethune & Vicinity	01/10/1916	08/10/1916
War Diary	Bethune	09/10/1916	09/10/1916
War Diary	Olville	11/10/1916	11/10/1916
War Diary	Thievres	17/10/1916	18/10/1916
War Diary	Authie	18/10/1916	18/10/1916
War Diary	Thievres	19/10/1916	19/10/1916
War Diary	Thievres & Authie	17/10/1916	31/10/1916
Heading	Confidential War Diary Of 31st Divisional Ammunition Column. From November 1st 1916 To November 30th 1916. (Volume XI)		
War Diary	Thievres & Authie	01/11/1916	21/11/1916
War Diary	Bayencourt	21/11/1916	21/11/1916

War Diary	Thievres Authie		21/11/1916	21/11/1916
War Diary	Dumpsat Coigneux Bayencourt	22/11/1916	29/11/1916
War Diary	Thievres	29/11/1916	30/11/1916
Heading	Confidential War Diary of 31st Divisional Ammunition Column. From 1st December 1916 To 31st December 1916. Volume XII		
War Diary	Authie	01/12/1916	31/12/1916
War Diary	Famechon	01/12/1916	31/12/1916
Heading	Confidential War Diary Of 31st Divisional Ammunition Column. From 1st January 1917 To 31st January 1917. Volume XIII		
Miscellaneous	H Qrs 31st Div Arty	02/01/1917	02/01/1917
War Diary	Authie & Famechen	01/01/1917	16/01/1917
War Diary	Bayencourt	12/01/1917	12/01/1917
War Diary	Authie & Famechen	15/01/1917	15/01/1917
War Diary	Coigneux	16/01/1917	16/01/1917
War Diary	Hem	17/01/1917	31/01/1917
War Diary	Hem & Hardinval	16/01/1917	31/01/1917
Heading	Confidential War Diary Of 31st Divisional Ammunition Column. From 1st February 1917 To 28th Feby. 1917. Volume XIV		
War Diary	Hem & Hardinval	01/02/1917	01/02/1917
War Diary	St-Ouen	01/02/1917	09/02/1917
War Diary	Bouzincourt	14/02/1917	20/02/1917
War Diary	St Ouen	20/02/1917	20/02/1917
War Diary	Famechon	21/02/1917	21/02/1917
War Diary	Bouzincourt	25/02/1917	25/02/1917
War Diary	Coigneux & Authie	26/02/1917	26/02/1917
War Diary	Thieves Authie Famechen	25/02/1917	28/02/1917
Miscellaneous	H.Qrs 31st Div. Arty	28/02/1917	28/02/1917
Heading	Confidential. War Diary Of 31st Divisional Ammunition Column. From 1st March 1917 To 31st March 1917		
Miscellaneous	A Form Messages And Signals	31/03/1917	31/03/1917
War Diary	Thievres Authie Famechon	01/03/1917	05/03/1917
War Diary	St Leger	05/03/1917	05/03/1917
War Diary	Coigneux	06/03/1917	06/03/1917
War Diary	Sailly Au Bois	10/03/1917	10/03/1917
War Diary	Bus	09/03/1917	09/03/1917
War Diary	Coigneux	11/03/1917	17/03/1917
War Diary	Bus	20/03/1917	20/03/1917
War Diary	Coigneux Bus & Sailly	05/03/1917	20/03/1917
War Diary	Hem	20/03/1917	20/03/1917
War Diary	Occoches	20/03/1917	20/03/1917
War Diary	Aubrometz	21/03/1917	21/03/1917
War Diary	Bergueneuse	22/03/1917	23/03/1917
War Diary	Hallicourt	24/03/1917	24/03/1917
War Diary	St Floris	25/03/1917	25/03/1917
War Diary	Camblain L'Abbe	25/03/1917	31/03/1917
War Diary	St Floris	25/03/1917	31/03/1917
Heading	Confidential War Diary Of 31st Divisional Ammunition Column. From 1st April 1917 To 30th April 1917. Volume XVI		
War Diary	Camblain L'Abbe	01/04/1917	13/04/1917
War Diary	Maroeuil	13/04/1917	13/04/1917
War Diary	Anzin-St Aubin	13/04/1917	30/04/1917
War Diary	Lagnngoy Magnicourt	01/04/1917	30/04/1917

Heading	Confidential War Diary Of 31st Divisional Ammunition Column. From 1st May To 31st May 1917. Volume XVII		
War Diary	Maroueil	01/05/1917	07/05/1917
War Diary	Anzin	20/05/1917	22/05/1917
Heading	Confidential War Diary Of 31st Divisional Ammunition Column. From 1st June 1917 To 30th June 1917. Volume XVIII		
Miscellaneous	H.Qrs 31st. Div. Arty.	30/06/1917	30/06/1917
War Diary	Anzin-St Aubin	01/06/1917	30/06/1917
War Diary	G.11b.5.1 Sheet-51 BNW	12/06/1917	19/06/1917
Heading	Confidential War Diary Of 31st Divisional Ammunition Column. From 1st July To 31st July, 1917. Volume XIX		
War Diary	Anzin St Aubin & Mont St Eloi	01/07/1917	31/07/1917
War Diary	Arras-Bailleul Road G.11 B.5.1 Map 51B N.W.	05/07/1917	18/07/1917
War Diary	Front St Eloi	18/07/1917	20/07/1917
War Diary	La Targette B7 & T26 Map Ref Petit Vimy 1/20000	20/07/1917	20/07/1917
War Diary	Map Ref Petit Vimy 1/20000	26/07/1917	26/07/1917
Heading	Confidential War Diary Of 31st Divisional Ammunition Column. From 1st August To 31st August, 1917. Volume XX		
Miscellaneous	H.Qrs. 31st Div Arty	31/08/1917	31/08/1917
War Diary	La Targette & Mt St Eloi	01/08/1917	31/08/1917
War Diary	Front St Eloi	01/08/1917	31/08/1917
Heading	Confidential War Diary Of 31st Divisional Ammunition Column. From 1st Sept. To 30th Sept. 1917. Volume XXI		
Miscellaneous	HQ 31st Div. Arty.	30/09/1917	30/09/1917
War Diary	Int St Eloi	01/09/1917	01/09/1917
War Diary	La Targette A.R.P.	01/09/1917	06/09/1917
War Diary	Int St Eloi	11/09/1917	11/09/1917
War Diary	La Targette A.R.P	11/09/1917	11/09/1917
War Diary	Madagascar A 26.d & A 27 A.	11/09/1917	11/09/1917
War Diary	G.11 Central Map Ref 51 B N.W.	20/09/1917	30/09/1917
Heading	Confidential War Diary Of 31st Divisional Ammunition Column. From 1st October To 31st October, 1917 Volume XXII		
Heading	HQ 31st Div Arty	31/10/1917	31/10/1917
War Diary	Ecurie	01/10/1917	24/10/1917
War Diary	Madagascar	24/10/1917	31/10/1917
Heading	Confidential War Diary Of 31st Divisional Ammunition Column. From 1st November To 30th November, 1917 Volume XXIII		
Miscellaneous	H Qrs 31st Div Arty	01/12/1917	01/12/1917
War Diary	Madagascar	01/11/1917	30/11/1917
War Diary	G.11.b.23 Map Ref 51b N.W. 1/20000	30/11/1917	30/11/1917
Heading	Confidential War Diary Of 31st Divisional Ammunition Column. From 1st December To 31st December 1917. Volume XXIV		
Heading	HQ 31st Div Arty	31/12/1917	31/12/1917
War Diary	Anzin Madagascar Road	01/12/1917	31/12/1917
War Diary	G.11.b.2.3 Map Ref. 51b N.W.	23/12/1917	23/12/1917
Heading	Confidential War Diary Of 31st Divisional Ammunition Column. From 1st January To 31st January 1918 Volume XXV		

Miscellaneous	H Qrs 31st Div Arty	31/01/1918	31/01/1918
War Diary	Madagascar	01/01/1918	31/01/1918

Heading: Confidential War Diary Of 31st Divisional Ammunition Column. From 1st February To 28th February 1918. Volume XXVI

War Diary	Madagascar	01/02/1918	28/02/1918

Heading: Confidential War Diary Of 31st Divisional Ammunition Column. From 1st March 1918 To 31st March 1918

War Diary	Madagascar	01/03/1918	06/03/1918
War Diary	Gauchin Legal	22/03/1918	22/03/1918
War Diary	Bavincourt	23/03/1918	23/03/1918
War Diary	Douchy-les-Ayettes	24/03/1918	26/03/1918
War Diary	Monchy Area	26/03/1918	26/03/1918
War Diary	Gaudiempre	26/03/1918	31/03/1918

Heading: 31st Division 31st Divisional Ammunition Column. April 1918

Heading: Confidential War Diary Of 31st Divisional Ammunition Column. From 1st April To 30th April, 1918 Volume XXVIII

Miscellaneous	H.Qrs. 31st Div. Arty.	02/05/1918	02/05/1918
War Diary	Gaudiempre	01/04/1918	01/04/1918
War Diary	Pommier	06/04/1918	06/04/1918
War Diary	St Amand	09/04/1918	09/04/1918
War Diary	Gaudiempre	26/04/1918	30/04/1918

Heading: Confidential War Diary Of 31st Divisional Ammunition Column. From 1st May To 31st May, 1918 Volume XXIX

War Diary	Gaudiempre	01/05/1918	31/05/1918

Heading: Confidential War Diary Of 31st Divisional Ammunition Column. From 1st June To 30th June 1918 Volume XXX

War Diary	Humbercourt	01/06/1918	14/06/1918
War Diary	Gaudiempre	15/06/1918	15/06/1918
War Diary	Gaudiempre & Pommiers	15/06/1918	25/06/1918
War Diary	Gaudiempre	26/06/1918	26/06/1918
War Diary	Mondicourt	27/06/1918	28/06/1918
War Diary	Berguette Aire	28/06/1918	28/06/1918
War Diary	La Belle Hotesse	29/06/1918	30/06/1918

Heading: Confidential War Diary Of 31st Divisional Ammunition Column. From 1st July To 31st July, 1918 Volume XXXI

Miscellaneous	HQ 31st Div. Arty	31/07/1918	31/07/1918
War Diary	La Belle Hotesse	01/07/1918	02/07/1918
War Diary	Sercus	03/07/1918	03/07/1918
War Diary	Bois des Huit Rues	03/07/1918	03/07/1918
War Diary	Sercus	03/07/1918	31/07/1918

Heading: Confidential War Diary Of 31st Divisional Ammunition Column. From 1st August To 31st August 1918. Volume XXXII

Miscellaneous	HQ 31st Div Arty	31/08/1918	31/08/1918
War Diary	Sercus	01/08/1918	30/08/1918
War Diary	Hallow Cappel	27/08/1918	27/08/1918
War Diary	Lynde	29/08/1918	29/08/1918
War Diary	Longue Croix	30/08/1918	30/08/1918
War Diary	Sercus	31/08/1918	31/08/1918
War Diary	Bois des Sheet Ref	31/08/1918	31/08/1918

War Diary	Le Crinchon	31/08/1918	31/08/1918
Heading	Confidential War Diary Of 31st Divisional Ammunition Column. From 1st September To 30th September, 1918. Volume XXXIII		
Miscellaneous	H.Q 31st Div Arty	30/09/1918	30/09/1918
War Diary	Le Crinchon (Sheet 36 A)	01/09/1918	02/09/1918
War Diary	Vieux Berquin	03/09/1918	03/09/1918
War Diary	(Sheet 36 A)	03/09/1918	10/09/1918
War Diary	Sheet Morris 2a 1/20000	11/09/1918	30/09/1918
Heading	Confidential War Diary Of 31st Divisional Ammunition Column. From 1st October To 31st October, 1918. Volume XXXIV		
Miscellaneous	HQ 31 Div Arty	01/11/1918	01/11/1918
War Diary		01/10/1918	31/10/1918
Heading	Confidential War Diary Of 31st Divisional Ammunition Column. From 1st November To 30th November, 1918. Volume XXXV		
Miscellaneous	HQ 31st Div Arty	01/12/1918	01/12/1918
War Diary		01/11/1918	30/11/1918
Heading	Confidential War Diary Of 31st Divisional Ammunition Column. From 1st December To 31st December 1918 Volume XXXVI		
Miscellaneous	HQ 31st Div Arty	31/12/1918	31/12/1918
War Diary	Hallines	01/12/1918	07/12/1918
War Diary	Esquerdes	07/12/1918	31/12/1918
Heading	Confidential War Diary Of 31st Divisional Ammunition Column. From 1st January To 31st January 1919 Volume XXXVII		
War Diary		01/01/1919	31/01/1919
Heading	Confidential War Diary Of 31st Divisional Ammunition Column. From 1st February To 28th February 1919. Volume XXXVIII		
War Diary	Esquerdes	01/02/1919	28/02/1919
War Diary	St Dunstans	01/02/1919	28/02/1919
Heading	Confidential War Diary Of 31st Divisional Ammunition Column. From 1st March To 31st March, 1919. Volume XXXIX		
War Diary	Esquerdes	20/03/1919	20/03/1919
Heading	Confidential War Diary Of 31st Divisional Ammunition Column. From 1st April To 30th April, 1919 Volume XL		
War Diary	Esquerdes	01/04/1919	30/04/1919

WO95/23521
Div Amn Column
Apr '16 - Feb '19

31ST DIV'L AMM'N COL'
APR 1916-APR 1919

31ST DIVISION
DIV'L ARTILLERY

WAR DIARY or INTELLIGENCE SUMMARY.
(Erase heading not required.)

Army Form C. 2118.

31st Div'l Signal Coy
Lt Col F.J. Boring R.E.
Comdg

Place	Date	Hour	Summary of Events and Information	Remarks and references to Appendices
			April 1916	
Marseilles	3rd		Arrival Marseilles – Disembark same day	NO CASUALTIES
"	4th		Duration Voyage from Alexandria 6 Days. During voyage NUMBER 8 to No 3 ES	
			Entrained – No 1 Section for Doullens	
			HQrs remainder Unit - for Abbeville	
Abbeville	5th		No 1 Section arrives at Doullens	
Doullens	6th		HQrs, No 2, No 3 Sect arrive & detrain Abbeville	
Amplier	6th		HQrs, No 2, No 3 Sect march from Doullens to Amplier	
Abbeville	7th		No 1 Sect marches from Abbeville with 89 Bgde & reports	
			Bivouacs at Candas.	
Amplier	8th		No 1 Sect arrives at Amplier - no Casualties on march -	
			very two halts, nightly. New Harness & animals rally prettily broken	
			Capt R. Digby Owens OC No 1 Sect reported as evicted to No 2 Sect from Abbeville	
			on 6-4-16	
Thièvres	11th		Column marches from Amplier to Thièvres - takes up Billets & Bivouacs	
	14th		Column marches from Sus Per R to War Establishment	
			fills up with Animals from Sus Per R to War Establishment	

Army Form C. 2118.

WAR DIARY
or
INTELLIGENCE SUMMARY.
(Erase heading not required.)

31st Div:l Amm:n Col
Lt Col J. Dixon R.F.A. Comdg

April 1916

Place	Date	Hour	Summary of Events and Information	Remarks and references to Appendices
Thièvres	27th		Capt R Digby Mens OC No 1 Sect:n Invalided England & Struck off Strength	
"	14th		Fitting Harness - Shoeing - Teaming & Training whilst -	
"	15		awaiting Details from Base to complete Establishment.	
	30th			

WAR DIARY or INTELLIGENCE SUMMARY

Army Form C. 2118.

31st Div. Amm'n Col
Lt/Col J. Oshoring R.F.A Com'd'g

Place	Date	Hour	Summary of Events and Information	Remarks and references to Appendices
			May 1916	
Thièvres	1st		Commence Supply of Amm'n to B.A.C's	
"	3rd		{Lt. J. A" J. M. Main takes Command of that Sect'n — Lt. W.S. Higgins takes up duties of ADJ't}	
"	15th		Final Draft from Base (46 Drivers) completes Establishment	
"	15th		{ NEW ESTABLISHMENT of COLUMN } G.H.Q letter N° O.B. 818/28-4-16	
			(B.A.C's merged into D.A.C)	
			N°3. HQrs — N°'s 1, 2, 3 Sect'ns "A" Echelon } West : 16 Officers - 818 O.R's	
			N°4 Sect. "B" Echelon } 90 Riders 968 L.D's	
			(15 suphers Officers attached)	
			HQrs "B" Echelon remain at Thièvres	
Authie	15th		N°'s 1, 2, 3 (mobile) Sect'ns "A" Echelon formed + Billeted at Authie.	
Thièvres	16th		Hand over to 48th Div Amm Col — 40 teams of mules & 8 rivers fully equipped	
"	23rd		Capt M.A. Archibald L. "A" R.A Summers - Transferred to 4th Div. H.T.M Batt's	
"	24th		Appointment of Lt W.S. Higgins as ADJ't Column made definite Authority HQ 4th Army VIIIth Corps	
"	28th		Evacuate - to Advanced Horse Transport Depot Abbeville. 35 P. Shoeing s. 2 Wheelers	
	29th		to 113th H. Batt'y R.F.A — 5 P. Shoeing s. + 1 Wheeler H.T.M to 21st Div.	
Authie	29th		Capt. J.J. Haney R.F.A J. 2 /1st L.H. 20 June posted to V/31 H.T.M Batt'y	
Thièvres	1st to 31st		Training and amalgamation of B.A.C's into D.A.C. Very effective - No interruption from Supply During Change of Training	

WAR DIARY
or
INTELLIGENCE SUMMARY

Army Form C. 2118.

June

31st D.A.C.

Vol 3

JUNE 1916

Place	Date	Hour	Summary of Events and Information	Remarks and references to Appendices
Thiènes Aulnes Bus Wood	1 to 7 8th 8th	}	Routine Work & Supply of Ammⁿ. Sections 1, 2, 3 of A. Echelon to move Bus Wood	
Thiènes Bus Wood	8th 22nd	}	Supply of Ammunition	
Bus Wood	22nd		HQ. moved from Thiènes to Bus Wood	
Bus Wood	26th		2nd Enemy Aeroplanes drop Bombs in Wood - no Damage. Supply of Ammⁿ & Shrapnel from 1st to 30th.	

J. Dutois
Lt Col R.F.A
Comm^{dg} 31st DAC

31st DIVISIONAL AMMUNITION COLUMN R.F.A.

1st to 31st JULY 1916.

WAR DIARY

Confidential

War Diary

of

3rd Divn: Ammn: Col:

1st July to 31st July
1916.

Vol no 4

WAR DIARY or INTELLIGENCE SUMMARY.

(Erase heading not required.)

Army Form C. 2118.

31st D.A.C. July 1916. Volume VII

Place	Date	Hour	Summary of Events and Information	Remarks and references to Appendices
Bus	1st	-	**July 1916** Bus Word (HQ "A" Echelon) Shelled from 12.30 am to 5.15 am. Horses & men removed to safety — Casualties: One horse.	
Oeceches	6th	-	"B" Echelon march from Thièvres to Oeceches	
B.1.5	7th	-	Horses & men Ave Lieutenant Rump.	
Oeceches	8th	-	HQ "A" Echelon march from Bus to Oeceches	
Thièvres	9th	-	Column march by Sections to Auxi-le-Château, Fréventi-Conteville & proceed	
Janval	10th	-	by Rail to Thièvres & Janval.	
			HQ "A" Echelon march from Tenniey to Guix Trévaimise	
Guix trévaimise	15th	-	1 Officer with 12 Majors, interpersonnel detached to 5th Anzac Div.Coly.	
	16th	-	1 Officer with 12 Majors lent to 5th Anzac Div.Coly & 1 officer + 12 men to 5th Anzac Coly.	
	21st	-	"B" Echelon march from Thièvres to Guix Trévaimise	
	25th	-		

Normal Supplies of Ammunition throughout this period.

JBThompson Bd Coll R.F.A
Commanding 31st D.A.C.

CONFIDENTIAL.

WAR DIARY

OF

31st DIVL. AMMN. COLUMN.

From AUGUST 1st 1916 to AUGUST 31st 1916.

VOLUME VIII

Volume VIII

August 1916

WAR DIARY or INTELLIGENCE SUMMARY.

31st Div¹ Amm'n Column

Army Form C. 2118.

Place	Date	Hour	Summary of Events and Information	Remarks and references to Appendices
Gras Huorance	1st to 12th		Normal Supply of Ammunition	
"	13th to 18th		X, Y, Z MTM Batt's & V³¹ H.T.M Batt'y attached to DAC. Normal Supply of Ammunition	
"	19th to 30th		No 3 Sect'n DAC attached to 61st Div Art'y. No 3 Sect'n DAC 30th Div Art'y attached to 31st DAC	
"	31st		Normal Supply of Ammunition	

V.J. Diering
Lieut.R.F.A.
Comd'g 31st DAC

CONFIDENTIAL.

WAR DIARY

OF

3/1st Wilts Ammn Column

From 1st September 1916 to 30th September 1916.

(VOLUME IX)

Vol 6

WAR DIARY 31st D.A.C.

September 1916

Army Form C. 2118

INTELLIGENCE SUMMARY

Place	Date	Hour	Summary of Events and Information	Remarks and references to Appendices
Auxy-haut-mcul	1st to 18th		Normal Supply of Ammⁿ	
Bethune	18th		Take over 30th D.A.C Dumps	
Bethune	19th		HQ'rs N°s 1 & 2 Sect'ns "A" Echelon, & "B" Echelon move from Auxy-haut-mcul to Bethune	
Bethune	19th to 30th		Normal Supply of Ammⁿ	

J.P. Strong Lt Col R.F.A.
Comd'g 31st D.A.C.

Confidential

WAR DIARY

OF

31st DIVISIONAL AMMUNITION COLUMN.

From 1st OCTOBER 1916 to 31st OCTOBER 1916.

VOLUME X

Vol 7

31st Div'l Amm Col

WAR DIARY or INTELLIGENCE SUMMARY

Army Form C. 2118.

October 1916

Place	Date	Hour	Summary of Events and Information	Remarks and references to Appendices
Béthune & Vicinity	Oct-1st to 8th		HQrs "A" & "B" Echelon. Normal Supply of Ammn (1st Army XI Corps)	
Béthune	9th		HQr Nos 1 & 2 Sections "A" Echelon move from Béthune & Vicinity to Orville No 3 Section "A" Echelon move from Brux mines to Orville No 4 Section "B" Echelon move from Verdrel - Béthune to Thièvres	
Orville	11th		HQ, 1st Army XIII Corps to 4th Reserve Army XIII Corps	
"	"		HQrs Nos 1,2,3 Sec"s "A" Ech'n move from Orville to Thièvres All 18p: 8.7 & 4.5" Q.F majors handed from Orville to 31st Div Arty also 26 B.S majors handed from Thièvres to 31st Div Arty	
Thièvres	17th		Take over Amm Dump from "N" NAC at Couin/Croix all Q.F majors (18p: 2.4 & 5"How) & 26 B.S majors returned from NAC Dump to Amm on 1,2,3 Sec'ns "A" Echelon move from Thièvres to Authie	
Authie	"		Take over "Amm Dump" at Bus from 51st DAC	
Thièvres	18th		Handover Bus "Amm Dump" to HQ's DAC & take over Forceville Dump (Bayencourt) from 19 DAC	
Thièvres/Authie	11th to 31st		Normal Supply of Ammn	

H. Brig General RFA
Co-op.g. 31st DAC

CONFIDENTIAL.

WAR DIARY

OF

31st DIVISIONAL AMMUNITION COLUMN.

From November 1st 1916. to November 30th 1916.

(VOLUME XI)

WAR DIARY or INTELLIGENCE SUMMARY

Army Form C. 2118.

November 1916   3rd A.A.C   Volume XI

Place	Date	Hour	Summary of Events and Information	Remarks and references to Appendices
Thievres	1st to 21st	—	Annual Supply of Ammunition	
Bayencourt	21st	—	Taken over 3rd Div Dump	
Thievres	21st (22nd to 29th)	—	Annual Supply of Ammunition; Engineers Rum Salt Reinforcements	
Thievres	29th	—	Move N° 4 Sect "B" Echelon to Famechon	
Thievres	30th	—	H.Q. & 3rd A.A.C move to Authie	

[signatures]

CONFIDENTIAL.

WAR DIARY

OF

31st DIVISIONAL AMMUNITION COLUMN.

From 1st DECEMBER 1916 to 31st DECEMBER 1916.

VOLUME XII.

Vol 9

WAR DIARY or INTELLIGENCE SUMMARY

December 1916 — 31st Div. Ammn Col.

Army Form C. 2118. Volume XII

Place	Date	Hour	Summary of Events and Information	Remarks and references to Appendices
Authie	1st / 31st			
Famechon	1st / 31st	"A" Echelon normal supply of Ammn.		
		"B" Echelon normal supply of Ammn.		
			P. Skene Lt Col RFA Comdg 31st D.A.C	

CONFIDENTIAL.

WAR DIARY

OF

31st DIVISIONAL AMMUNITION COLUMN.

FROM 1st JANUARY 1917 TO 31st JANUARY 1917.

VOLUME XIII.

Q 285 —

Mr Payne
31st Air City

Herewith diary
diary for January 1917
for Air unit under my
command.

J.T. Babington
Commdg. 3rd Wing

2/2

WAR DIARY or INTELLIGENCE SUMMARY.
(Erase heading not required.)

31st D.A.C.
Army Form C. 2118.
Volume XIII

January 1917

Place	Date	Hour	Summary of Events and Information	Remarks and references to Appendices
Quilhi 8 Frenchun	1st to 10th		Normal Supply of Amm".	
Bayencourt Frenchun	12th to 14th		Run 6 Sitn handed over to 19th Div.	
Authie	15th		"A" Echelon move to HEM - "B" Echelon move to HARDINVAL	
Coigneux	16th		Amm" Dumps handed over to 19th Div.	
Hem	17th		10ft 50 OR's Detached with 19th DAC at COIGNEUX to extend Dump Reorganisation of DAC into 2 Sectns ("A" Echelon) + "B" Echelon curtailed.	
"	20th		2 offrs, 70 OR's, 116 animals. Six 18pdrs B.7, Two 4.5 How wgs. 243 wgs (complete with ammn) 8, 18 SAA (Tett Stores) Transferred to A.F.A. By "A" Queen Col.	
Hem	21st		Surplus personnel, vehicles + animals from 165,169,170 Bys & 517 How By to hampenea to DAC (31st)	
Hem	26th		Two 4.5 How Wgs, Two P5 Wgs 24 LD animals & 12 N"hamptens" to D/311 Bys RFA	
Hem	27th		Two 4.5 How Wgs, Two P5 Wgs 24 LD animals & 12 N"hamptens" to D/155 By R.F.A	
"	28th		Eleven P5 animals & 12 O draught to II S.A.A Sectn from 7th Div.	
Hem	30th		2 B"r 2 SS, 22 N"r, Six 18pdr Q.F. 3rd + 5 How Wg (with ammn) 38 SMy N"hamptens to 14th H.A By C	
Hem	31st		Surplus Amm". + Equipm"t. By sM ("hanving pers pura only, harning, spare & oil -	
Authie	16 to 30th		sg. Brewer- Lt Col - comm"g 31st D.A.C.	

T2134. Wt. W708-776. 500000. 4/15. Sir J.C. & S.

CONFIDENTIAL.

WAR DIARY

OF

31st DIVISIONAL AMMUNITION COLUMN.

From 1st February 1917 to 28th Feby. 1917.

VOLUME XIV.

WAR DIARY or INTELLIGENCE SUMMARY

31st Div Amm Col Army Form C. 2118.
February 1917. Volume XIV

Place	Date	Hour	Summary of Events and Information	Remarks and references to Appendices
Hersin	1st			
Houchin				
St Ouen	12th	11 gh	Column moves to St Ouen - (by Road)	
Do	13th	9 A	General Fatigues - Transfer in Corps & Division	
Regiment	14th	9 A	Column leaves S.A.A Sect" marches to Boujigincourt & attached to 18th Div Hq.	
Do		9.20h	Delivers 2368 Rds S.A.A Amm to 170th Bde R.F.A at Thiepval	
St Ouen	20th		General Fatigues & Transport to 18th Div" & Brigade's 31st Div	
	January 21st		S.A.A Sect" marches from St Ouen to Famechon	
Bonnegnant	25th		S.A.A Sect" arrives at Famechon	
Infantry	26th		"A" Sect" marches to Arthiz - No 2 Sect"y Hq" marches to Thiévres, "B" Bde to Famechon	
Arthuis			Takes over Dumps from 19th Div Hq	
Thiévres	25th			
Authie	26th			
Famechon	28th			

General Fatigues & Transport

G. Blurry Rhys H. R.F.A
Commdg 31st D.A.C.

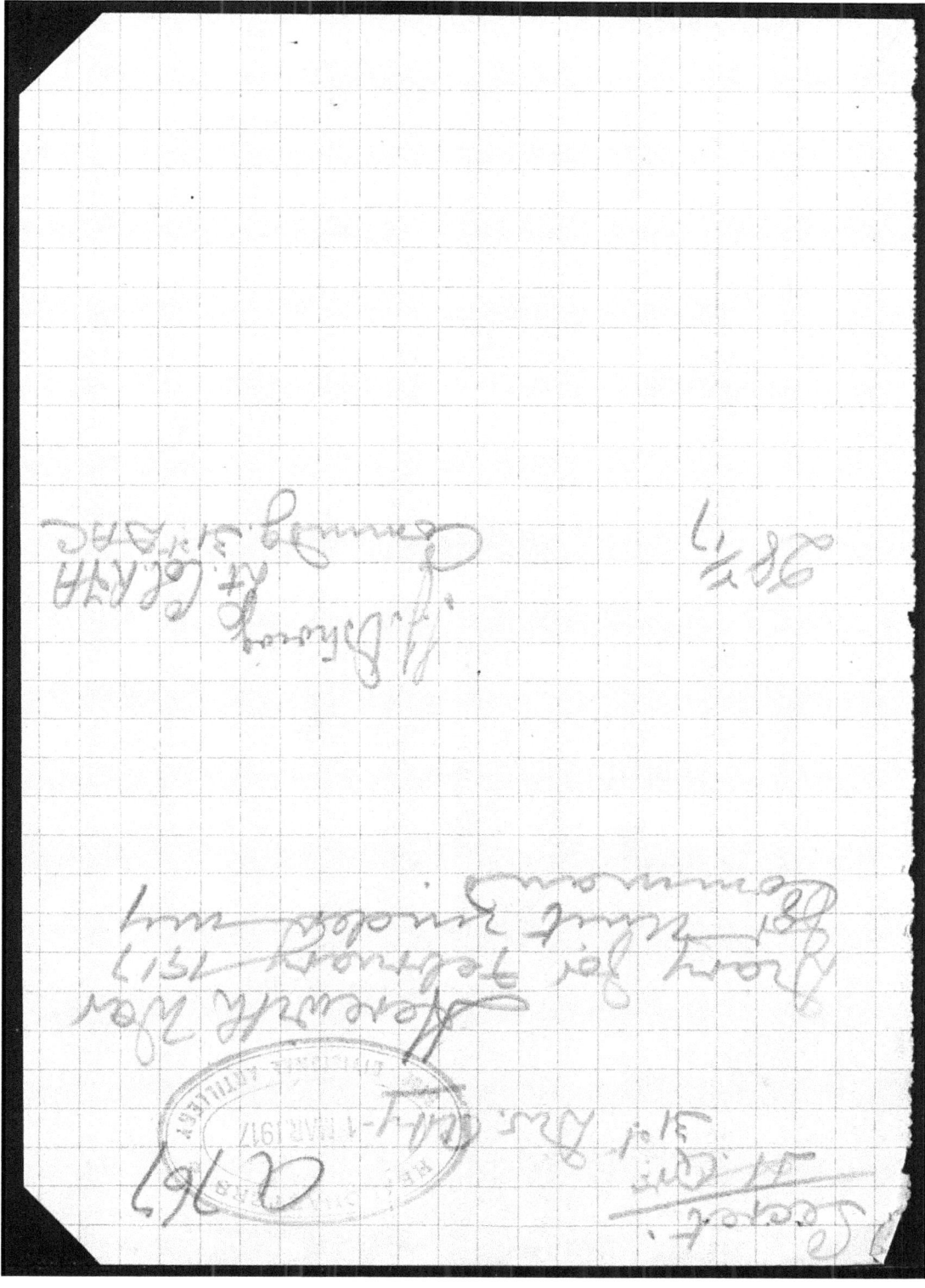

CONFIDENTIAL.

WAR DIARY

OF

31st DIVISIONAL AMMUNITION COLUMN.

From 1st MARCH 1917 to 31st MARCH 1917.

VOLUME XV.

MESSAGES AND SIGNALS.

TO HQ of the 31st Div Arty

Sender's Number.	Day of Month.	In reply to Number.	AAA
H 217	31/3	—	

Herewith 2/Lt
Report for March 1917 for
Unit under my Command.

H Finney Lt
Comdg 31st DAC

31/3/17

Page 1. — March 1917 —

WAR DIARY
31st D.A.C.
INTELLIGENCE SUMMARY.
(Erase heading not required.)

Army Form C. 2118.

1st March 1917 to 31st March 1917

Volume XV

Place	Date	Hour	Summary of Events and Information	Remarks and references to Appendices
Thièvres Authie Famechon	1st to 5th		Normal Supply of Amm'n & General Transport Work.	
St Leger	5th		HQrs DAC move from Thièvres to St Leger	
Grigneux	6th		No 2 Sect'n move from Thièvres to Grigneux	
Sailly-au-Bois	9th		No 1 Sect'n move from Authie to Sailly-au-Bois & establish forward Dumps	
Grigneux	10th		Take over Bus dump from 19th Div.	
Bus	9th		"B" Echelon move from Famechon to Grigneux	
Grigneux	11th		Hand over Grigneux Dump to 46th Div	
Bus	20th		Hand over Bus Dump to 11th Div	
Grigneux Bus & Sailly	5 to 20th		Normal Supply of Amm'n from Dumps { General Transport Work } ("A" Echelon) ("B" Echelon)	
Hem Occoches	20th		HQrs DAC & "B" Echelon march to Hem No1 & No2 Sections march to Occoches	
Autriment Bergueneuse	21st 22		HQrs "A" & "B" Echelons march to Autriment " " to Bergueneuse	
"	23rd		Rest at Bergueneuse	

Page II. March 1917 (cont'd)

WAR DIARY 31st D.A.C.

INTELLIGENCE SUMMARY
(Erase heading not required)

Army Form C. 2118.

Place	Date	Hour	Summary of Events and Information	Remarks and references to Appendices
Hallicourt	24th		HQrs "A" & "B" Echelons march from Bergnemeuse to Hallicourt	
St Floris	25th		S.A.A Sectn detached from 31st Div Att'd march to St Floris	
Cambrin	25th		HQrs "A" Echelon + "B" Echelon les S.A.A Sectn march from Hallicourt to Cambrin	
L'Atre	"		Above attached to 1st Canadian Div Arty	
			HQrs Cambrin & L'Atre	
Cambrin	25th to 31st		Supply of Amm'n to Battery Positions in Area West of 1st Canadian DAC	
L'Atre	25th to 31st			
St Floris	25th to 31st		S.A.A Sectn with 31st Div — (HQrs St Venant area) General Transport	

J. Diviner
Lieut R.F.A.
Comdg 31st D.A.C.

C O N F I D E N T I A L

W A R   D I A R Y

O F

31st DIVISIONAL AMMUNITION COLUMN.

From 1st April 1917 to 30th April 1917.

V O L U M E XVI.

WAR DIARY
or
INTELLIGENCE SUMMARY

April 1917 31st D.A.C. Volume XVI

Army Form C. 2118.

Place	Date	Hour	Summary of Events and Information	Remarks and references to Appendices
Gouy-en-Artois	1st to 13th		Supply of Amm'n to 1st Canadian Div Arty & 31st Div Arty under Orders 1st Canadian Div 2nd Arty Bde	
Francueil	13th		H.Q. W.T.C. move to Manevil	
Couin-St Amour	"		No 1 & 2 Sections move to Couin-St Amour	
"	15th		From Gun dumps at G.9.B.2.3. Map Ref France 51 B N.W 1/20,000	
Couin-St Amour	17th		No 2 Section attached to 2nd Div	
"	"		No 1 Section attached to 63rd Div.	
"	18th		Supply of Amm'n	
"	13th to 30th		S.A.A Section (detached)	
Lahussoye	1st to		Transport & Tires, mis, Sundries to 31st Div	
Megulaine	30th			

M. Shorey Lt Col R.F.A.
Comdg 31st D.A.C.

C O N F I D E N T I A L.

W A R   D I A R Y.

O F

31st DIVISIONAL AMMUNITION COLUMN.

From 1st May to 31st May 1917.

V O L U M E XVII.

WAR DIARY
or
INTELLIGENCE SUMMARY.

(Erase heading not required.)

Army Form C. 2118.

3/7 Brigade Col
Volume XVII
1st-31st May 1917.

Instructions regarding War Diaries and Intelligence Summaries are contained in F. S. Regs., Part II. and the Staff Manual respectively. Title pages will be prepared in manuscript.

Place	Date	Hour	Summary of Events and Information	Remarks and references to Appendices
Morcourt	19/5		Took over A.P.9 from 63rd (R.N.) Division at Sq. 6 2.3 Arras 51.8 N.W.	
"	"		Headquarters 57.C. moved to Anzin de Arras.	
A.P.9	28/4		Switched A.P.9 at G 11 b 5.2. Arras 51.3 N.W.	
"	24/4		Handed over A.P.9 to G3 (R.N.) Division at G9b29T Arras 51.C.S.E.	

R.P. Reeds
Commanding
3rd Siamese Division R.F.A.

CONFIDENTIAL.

WAR DIARY

OF

31st DIVISIONAL AMMUNITION COLUMN.

From 1st June 1917 to 30th June 1917.

VOLUME XVIII.

SECRET

H.Q. 1/c
3rd Div.

Herewith Idea
Army for June 1917 for
Unit under my Command.

J.J. Finney
Lt. Col. RFA
Commdg. 3rd D.A.

30/7.

WAR DIARY or INTELLIGENCE SUMMARY

Army Form C. 2118.

June 1917 Volume XVIII

310th D.A.C. Army XVIII

Place	Date	Hour	Summary of Events and Information
Angin Staulin	1st to 30th		Normal Supply of Ammn
			Detail
	6.11 & 5.1		Shrapnel — Took over A.R.P. from 63rd (R.N) Div'n
	Shell/51 Bdy		
	2" T.M		Trench — Formed Dump for Salvaged Ammn

L.J. Diving
Lieut R.F.A.
Commdt 310 D.A.C.

30 JUN 1917
HEADQUARTERS
310th DIVISIONAL ARTILLERY

CONFIDENTIAL.

WAR DIARY

OF

31st DIVISIONAL AMMUNITION COLUMN.

From 1st July to 31st July, 1917.

VOLUME XIX.

WAR DIARY or INTELLIGENCE SUMMARY

Army Form C. 2118.
31st D.A.C. Volume IX

1st July 1917

Place	Date	Hour	Summary of Events and Information	Remarks and references to Appendices
Anzin St Aubin & Mont St Eloi	July 1st to 31st		Normal Supply of Ammunition Working Parties & Transport for Corps & Divn.	
Anzin - Boulleul Road	July 1st		Map 51B M.W	Detail as above
Mont St Eloi	July 5th		Handed over A.R.P. to 63rd Divn	
Mont St Eloi	July 18th		Handed over Salvaged Ammn Dump to 63rd Divn	
	July 18th		No 3 Sectn move to Mont St Eloi	
	July 20th		HQ's & No 3 & No 2 Sectns move to Mont St Eloi	
La Targette	July 20th		Take over ARP's from 1st Canadian Divn	
	July 26th		Handed over T26 ARP to 165 Bde R.F.A	

Lt. J. B....
Lt & Adjt 31st D.A.C

CONFIDENTIAL.

WAR DIARY

OF

31st DIVISIONAL AMMUNITION COLUMN.

From 1st August to 31st August, 1917.

VOLUME XX.

A 75

Die Stofe der Arbeit,

Hinweis über
Verlauf der Ausgrabungen der Funde
unter mir Kommando.

J.J. Nimmerfreh Gr. Rat
Commissa. S. a. Borg

31/8 17.

WAR DIARY
or
INTELLIGENCE SUMMARY

Army Form C. 2118.

31st Div. Amm. Colⁿ   Vol. XX

August 1917   From 1st to 31st August 1917

Place	Date	Hour	Summary of Events and Information	Remarks and references to Appendices
La Tourette } M. St Eloi } 1st to 31st M. St Eloi } 1st to 31st			Normal Supply of Ammn General Transport to fr Division.	

H.J. Oliving
Lieut R.F.A.
Commdg 31st D.A.C.

CONFIDENTIAL.

WAR DIARY

OF

31st DIVISIONAL AMMUNITION COLUMN.

From 1st Sept. to 30th Sept. 1917.

VOLUME XXI.

Secret.
H.Q.
3rd Res Army   QA/80
Herewith file 003
for Sept 1917, for work under
my Command.

[stamp: 30 SEP 1917]

H Browning
Brig. Gen. RA
Comdg, 3rd R.A.

30/9/17.

WAR DIARY or INTELLIGENCE SUMMARY

September 1917 — 31st D.A.C. — Army Form C. 2118.

Place	Date	Hour	Summary of Events and Information	Remarks and references to Appendices
Mt STELOI	1st to 10th		General Transport etc for Div.	
LA TARGETTE A.R.P.	10th to 11th	6	Normal Supply of Amm.	
Mt STELOI	11th		Handed over Standings to 3rd Canadian Div	
LA TARGETTE A.R.P.	11th	14	Handed over to 3rd Canadian Div.	
			Takeover Standings from 5th Div.	Mackay 404 A 26. Bty A 27 a. }11h
			Take over ARP from 5th Div	G.H. Cooled R 7½ A.S.84
			General Transport etc for Div + Normal Supply of Amm	Map 12-5/3 NW 3 1st to 30th

R.J. Downing
Lt Col RFA
Comm'g 31st DAC

30 SEP. 1917
31st DIVISIONAL ARTILLERY

WAR DIARY or INTELLIGENCE SUMMARY.

(Erase heading not required.)

CONFIDENTIAL.

WAR DIARY

OF

31st DIVISIONAL AMMUNITION COLUMN.

From 1st October to 31st October, 1917.

VOLUME XXII.

Army Form C. 2118.

Herewith War Diary for October, for Unit under my Command.

J.J. Sturm
Commanding 33rd RVH
31/10/17

M.C. 31st Division 331

31 OCT 1917

WAR DIARY or INTELLIGENCE SUMMARY.
Army Form C. 2118.

1st to 31st October 1917

Place	Date	Hour	Summary of Events and Information	Remarks and references to Appendices
Ennetières	1st to 24th		Normal Supply of Ammunition. General Transport to Div'ns & erection of Winter lines	
Madagascar	24th		Move in to Winter Standings	
Madagascar	25th to 31st		Normal Supply of Ammunition. General Transport for Div'ns	

J.J. Brinning
Lieut Col
Commanding 30th D.A.C.

WAR DIARY or INTELLIGENCE SUMMARY

CONFIDENTIAL.

WAR DIARY

OF

31st DIVISIONAL AMMUNITION COLUMN.

From 1st November to 30th November, 1917.

VOLUME XXIII.

Army Form C. 2118.

Noted.

A.J.S.
31/12/17

Ready for 2nd 151 foretting under my command
Forwarded for

J.J.Murray
Col. Cmdg.
"Cornwall" 31st Dec

Vol. XXIII

WAR DIARY
or
INTELLIGENCE SUMMARY.

(Erase heading not required.)

31st D.A.

Army Form C. 2118.

November 1917

Place	Date	Hour	Summary of Events and Information	Remarks and references to Appendices
Ypres area	1st to 30th		Normal supply of ammunition. General transport for Division. Take over 21st Div A.R.P.	G.H.Q 23 Map Ref 1/40,000 28NW

J.A. Brown
Lieut. Col. R.F.A
Comdg 31st D.A.C

CONFIDENTIAL.

WAR DIARY

OF

31st DIVISIONAL AMMUNITION COLUMN

From 1st December to 31st December 1917.

VOLUME XXIV.

Recd.
AHQ 3rd Res Cbty -2 JUN 1919

Forwarded for Rec. 1917 for that
much of my Command.

A.D.C.
31/1/19

JHShirey Lt Col 13th
Commdg. 3rd RCC

WAR DIARY or INTELLIGENCE SUMMARY.
(Erase heading not required.)

Army Form C. 2118.

December 1917 31st D.A.C.

Vol XXIV

Place	Date	Hour	Summary of Events and Information	Remarks and references to Appendices
ANZIN — MADAGASCAR ROAD	1st to 31st		Normal Supply of Ammⁿ & General Transport to Division	
P. 11. f. 2. 3. MAP REF. 51B N.W	23rd on		Handed over A.R.P to 56th Divⁿ.	

H. Dharig
Lieut RFA
Com^g 31st D.A.C

HEADQUARTERS
-2 JAN 1918
31st DIVISIONAL ARTILLERY

WAR DIARY or INTELLIGENCE SUMMARY.

CONFIDENTIAL.

WAR DIARY

OF

31st DIVISIONAL AMMUNITION COLUMN.

From 1st January to 31st January, 1918.

VOLUME XXV.

Secret

3rd Bur. O/III.

Herewith War Diary
for January 1918 for Units
under my Command.

H.Birwood
Lt.Gen.GOC
Comdg. 1st ANZAC

27/1/18

HEADQUARTERS,
31ST D.A.Q.
No. Q 898
Date 31-1-18

310 D.A.C.

WAR DIARY January 1918

Volume XXV

Place	Date	Hour	Summary of Events and Information	Remarks and references to Appendices
"Niagara"	1st/31st		Normal supply of Ammunition. General Transport, Tendering for parties & Fatigues.	

J.F. Strong
Lieut RFA
Comdt 310 D.A.C.

WAR DIARY
or
INTELLIGENCE SUMMARY.

Army Form C. 2118.

CONFIDENTIAL.

WAR DIARY
OF
31st DIVISIONAL AMMUNITION COLUMN.

From 1st February to 28th February, 1918.

VOLUME XXVI.

WAR DIARY or INTELLIGENCE SUMMARY

31st D.A.C. February 1918

Army Form C. 2118.

Place	Date	Hour	Summary of Events and Information	Remarks and references to Appendices
Marjoen	1st to 28th		Normal Supply of Ammunition, General Transport, Providing Gun Portires.	

28 FEB 1918

F. Shiney
Lieut RFA
Comdg 31st D.A.C.

CONFIDENTIAL.

WAR DIARY

OF

31st DIVISIONAL AMMUNITION COLUMN.

From 1st March 1918 to 31st March 1918.

VOLUME XXVII.

WAR DIARY or INTELLIGENCE SUMMARY

Army Form C. 2118.

March 1918   **31st D.A.C**

Place	Date	Hour	Summary of Events and Information	Remarks and references to Appendices
Magnicourt	1st	5"	Indian personnel which arrived late on Feb. 28th Distributed to Section 5 inch in New W.O. Normal Supply of Ammn	
" "	15th		Normal Supply of Ammn	
" "	6th		Relieved by 62nd D.A.C. + move into G.H.Q. Reserve at Gauchin Legal.	
Gauchin Legal	22nd		Move to Bavincourt (6th Cdn S. 3rd Army)	
Bavincourt	23rd		Move to Douchy-les-Ayettes + Supply of Ammn to Batteries	
Douchy-les-Ayettes	24 to 26		Supply of Ammn to Batteries	
" "	26th		Move to Monchy Area	
Monchy Area	26th		Move to Gaudiempré	
Gaudiempré	26 to 31st		Supply of Ammn to Batteries	

J.J. Browning R.F.A.
Comm'g 31st D.A.C.

APRIL 1918

31st Divisional Ammunition Column

31st Division

CONFIDENTIAL.

WAR DIARY

OF

31st DIVISIONAL AMMUNITION COLUMN

From 1st April to 30th April, 1918.

VOLUME XXVIII

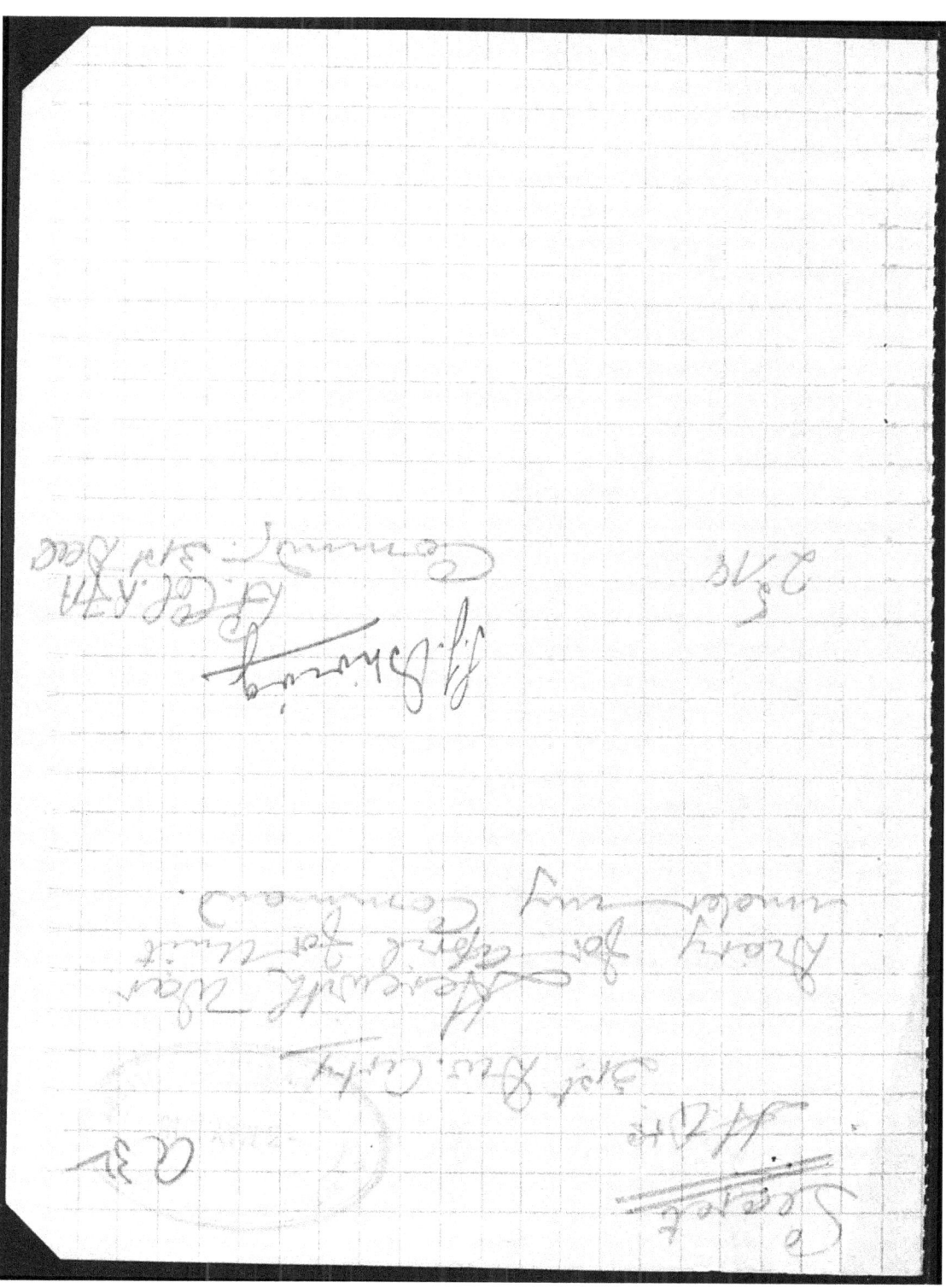

31st D.A.C.

WAR DIARY or INTELLIGENCE SUMMARY

April 1918

Army Form C. 2118.

Place	Date	Hour	Summary of Events and Information	Remarks and references to Appendices
Gauchempré	1st	-	"S.A.A. Sectn" move to Lucheux with Divn leaving S.A. Ammn on dump for 32nd Divn	
Gauchempré	10th		HQrs & No 1 & 2 Sectns ("A" Echelon) Attached to 32nd Divn.	
Pommier	6th		Handed over A.R.P. to 32nd Div.	
St Amand	9th		Formed A.R.P. at St Amand – Pommier Road	
Gauchempré	26th		HQ & No 1 & No 2 Sectns ("A" Echelon) attached to Guards Divn.	
Gauchempré	10th–30th		Normal supply of Ammn & in-Riding parties	

J.J. Shiving
Lt Col R.F.A.
Commdg 31st D.A.C.

CONFIDENTIAL.

WAR DIARY

OF

31st DIVISIONAL AMMUNITION COLUMN.

From 1st May to 31st May, 1918.

VOLUME XXIX.

WAR DIARY or INTELLIGENCE SUMMARY

Army Form C. 2118.

Vol. XXIX

MAY 1918   31st D.A.C.

Place	Date	Hour	Summary of Events and Information	Remarks and references to Appendices
Gorenflos	1st to 30th		Normal Supply of Amm. to Batteries.	
	30th	9.30am	Hdqrs No. 1 & 2 Section move to Fremboune	
	31st	Noon	Arrived at A.R.9.b.40.f.69	

1/6/18.

M Shining

Lt Col, R.a

Comdg 31st Div: Amm. Col.

[Stamp: HEADQUARTERS 2 JUN 1918 DIVISIONAL ARTILLERY]

CONFIDENTIAL.

WAR DIARY

OF

31st DIVISIONAL AMMUNITION COLUMN.

From 1st June to 30th June, 1918.

VOLUME XXX.

31st D.A.C.   WAR DIARY   JUNE 1918.   Vol XXX

Army Form C. 2118.

INTELLIGENCE SUMMARY
(Erase heading not required)

Place	Date	Hour	Summary of Events and Information	Remarks and references to Appendices
Humbercourt	1st to 14th		Rest –	
Gaudiempré	15th		Move to Gaudiempré & take over A.R.P. at Pommiers from Guards D.A.	
Gaudiempré & Pommiers	15th to 25th		Supply of Ammn & Transport	
Gaudiempré	26th		Hand over Pommiers A.R.Pt 2nd Divn & move to Humbercourt	
Humdicourt	27th & 28th		Leave Humbercourt & Entrain at Mondicourt & Doullens	
Berguette & Caire	28th		Detrain at Berguette & Caire & march to La Belle Hotesse to rejoin 31st Divn	
La Belle Hotesse	29th, 30th		Stand by.	

J.J. Schäning
Lt Col R.F.A.
Comdg 31st D.A.C.

CONFIDENTIAL.

WAR DIARY

OF

31st DIVISIONAL AMMUNITION COLUMN.

From 1st July to 31st July, 1918.

VOLUME XXXI.

Beirut.
3,U Rue Colas

Herewith the
Sorry for July for Simone's
reminder my Simone
Please.

H Johnny
At 6:15 pm
Coming at 8:00

31/78

WAR DIARY 31st D.A.C.

or INTELLIGENCE SUMMARY.
(Erase heading not required.)

Army Form C. 2118.

Vol. XXXI

JULY 1918

Place	Date	Hour	Summary of Events and Information	Remarks and references to Appendices
La Belle Hôtesse.	1st 2nd		At Rest & take over SAA Section at Wallon Cappelle.	
Sercus	3rd	HQ & no. 2 Sections taken over from 29th DAC		
Bois Jes	3rd	Take over ARP from 29th DAC		
Fruit Rues	3rd			
Sercus	3rd by 31st	Supply of Ammⁿ to Batteries.		

J. Skiving
Lt Col RFA
Cmdg 31st DAC

CONFIDENTIAL.

WAR DIARY

OF

31st DIVISIONAL AMMUNITION COLUMN.

From 1st August to 31st August, 1916.

VOLUME XXXII.

31/8/18

Memoing to the CEO AHA
Council 31 Aug

Health Officers
Report for the month of
August for their sunday
my Commons.

3rd Rec City [stamp: 31 AUG 1918]

Recd
H.G.

WAR DIARY or INTELLIGENCE SUMMARY

Army Form C. 2118.

Volume XXXII

August 1918

Place	Date	Hour	Summary of Events and Information	Remarks and references to Appendices
Senlis	1st		Further Ammunition to Batteries. Normal	
Vadencourt	30th		SOS fired. Normal	
Senlis	29th		do do do	
Longpré	30th		do do Longpré Gires	
			do do La Vicogne	
Senlis	31st		Hqrs No. 172 Batteries moved to the Brigade Hqrs	
			No. 1 Sec. B13 a 1.8.	
			No. 2 Sec. D1 e 5.0. Also 36ᵒ/hour	
Boves	"		O.P.9 moved to D10 d 8.0 Hqrs about 36ᵒ thrown	
Aubigny	"			
La Briche	"		Normal activity of Ammunition.	

A. Dering
Capt.
O.C. 3rd 79th

CONFIDENTIAL.

WAR DIARY

OF

31st DIVISIONAL AMMUNITION COLUMN.

From 1st September to 30th September, 1918.

VOLUME XXIII.

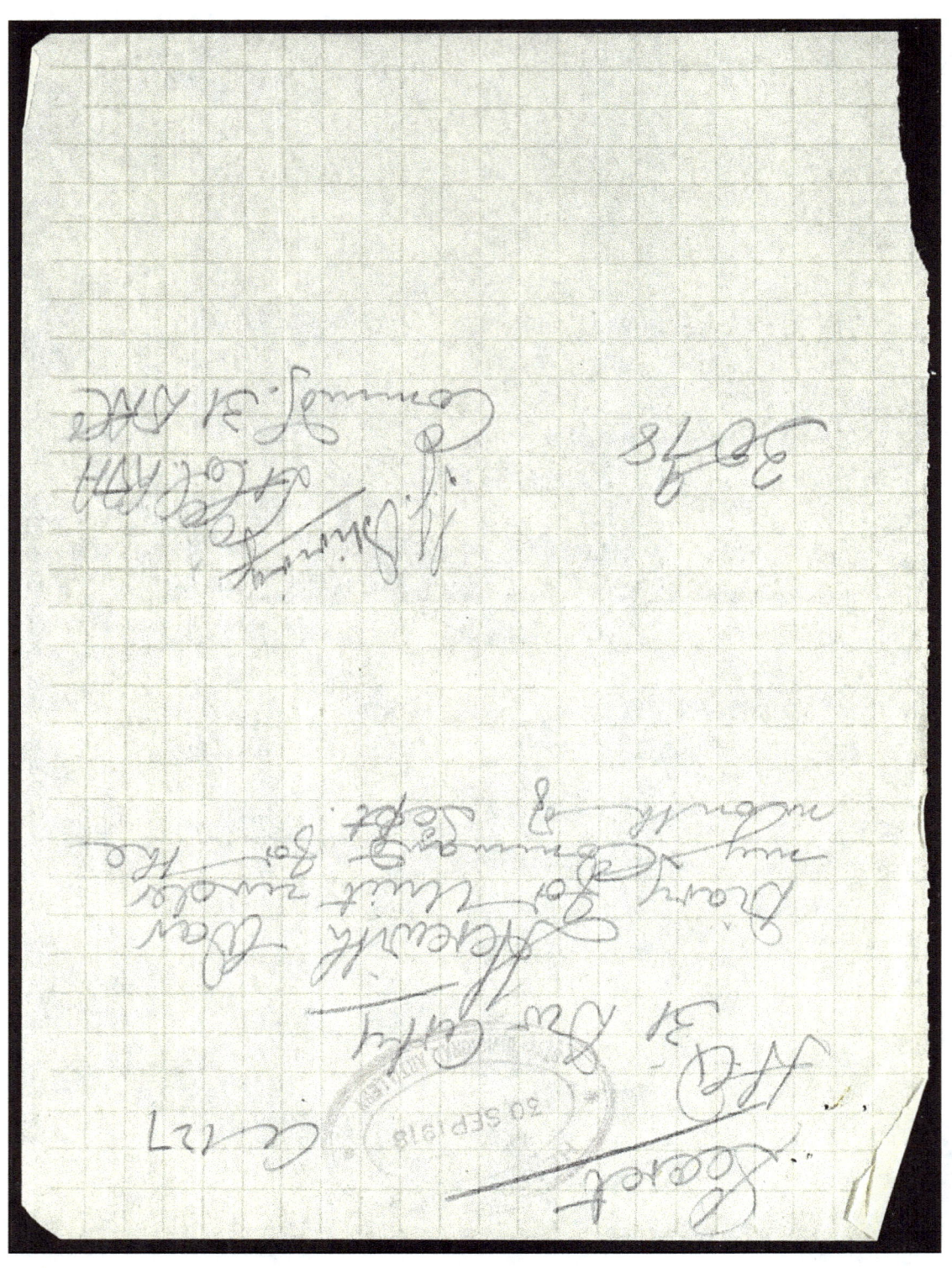

WAR DIARY or INTELLIGENCE SUMMARY

Army Form C. 2118.

31st D.A.C.

September 1918

(Erase heading not required.)

Place	Date	Hour	Summary of Events and Information	Remarks and references to Appendices
Le Cauchem (Sheet 36A)	1st/2nd		Normal Supply at "Amm" ARP formed at Vieux Berquin	
Vieux Berquin (Sheet 36A)	3rd		HQ's D 18.a.0.7 (near Hazebrouck - Au Souvenir) No 1 Sec'n E 19 Central (La Maquette) No 2 Sec'n E 9.C.3.8 (Petit Sec Bois)	
	4th 5th 6th 7th 8th 9th 10th		Salvage of Gun Amm" from Battles Normal Positions in 31st D.A. Area Gun Amm" 38115 - T.M 1032 - Vieux Berquin Dump handed over to 66th Div	
	10th		Move to following Locations HQ's A 2 C 9.1 No1 A 7 & 8.1 No2 A 2 & 9.1	
Shot hemis 2q ½ 11 am	11th		Take over 9th Div ARP on Bailleul - Armentières Road	
	11.15 14.00 30 10th to 30 10th to 30		Supply of Amm" to Batteries	
			3rd S.A.A Sec'n on Paris-Cashs Road Bailleul Area.	

J Diving Lieut RFA
Command'g 31st D.A.C.

CONFIDENTIAL.

WAR DIARY

OF

31st. Divisional Ammunition Column.

From 1st. October to 31st. October, 1918.

VOLUME XXXV

SECRET
Prestn.

To Dir arty.

Accounts for diesel for the month of October from this station my Command

8/11   Received Capt H.B Cannock R.E R.O

WAR DIARY or INTELLIGENCE SUMMARY

31st Divn Ammn Col — October 1918

Army Form C. 2118.

Vol. XXIV

Place	Date	Hour	Summary of Events and Information	Remarks and references to Appendices
Halt	Oct 15		No 11 Sec Hwe to 120 Central Sheet 28	
"	16		S.A.A. Sec do A.2.6.9 MERRIS 2"	
"	"		do S.29.a.43 Sheet 28	
"	17		do W.12.c.5" do	
"	"		Fward MR? See Tasks at WARNETON	
"	18		No 11 Sec Hwe to E.9.a.8.8 Sheet 36	
"	19		HQ? do W.25.a.4.2 " 28	
"	20		S.A.A. Sec do Croix Blanche " 30	
"	22		No 11 Sec do E.18.c.8.8 " 36	
"	23		S.A.A. Sec do ZANDVOORDE " 29	
"	24		HQ Sec do ZANDY " 29	
"	"		No 11 Sec do WATRELOS " do	
"	26		HQ Q? } do CUERNE " do	
"	"		No 2 Sec }	
"	"		No 11 Sec do HEULE " do	
"	27		S.A.A. Sec do CUERNE " do	
"	"		No 11 Sec do HARLEBEKE " do	

WAR DIARY
or
INTELLIGENCE SUMMARY.

Army Form C. 2118.

(Erase heading not required)

Place	Date	Hour	Summary of Events and Information	Remarks and references to Appendices
Morville	Oct 5.18		Dumps from H 20. 6 a & I 7. A (new) to I 17 c. 6 s – Sheet 29	
"	26/8		N°. 1 Sec. move to I 21 b. 9 s –	do
"	"		" II " do I 15 e. 2. 2	do
"	"		S.A.A. Sec. do I 7. a. 5. 6.	do
"	"		H.Q. D° do. J 21. D 7. 9	do
"	29/8			
"	31			

1.11.18

R Boulke Capt R.F.A.
Comdg 3°. O. O. A C

Instructions regarding War Diaries and Intelligence
Summaries are contained in F. S. Regs., Part II.
and the Staff Manual respectively. Title pages
will be prepared in manuscript.

CONFIDENTIAL.

WAR DIARY

OF

31st DIVISIONAL AMMUNITION COLUMN.

From 1st November to 30th November, 1918.

VOLUME XXXV.

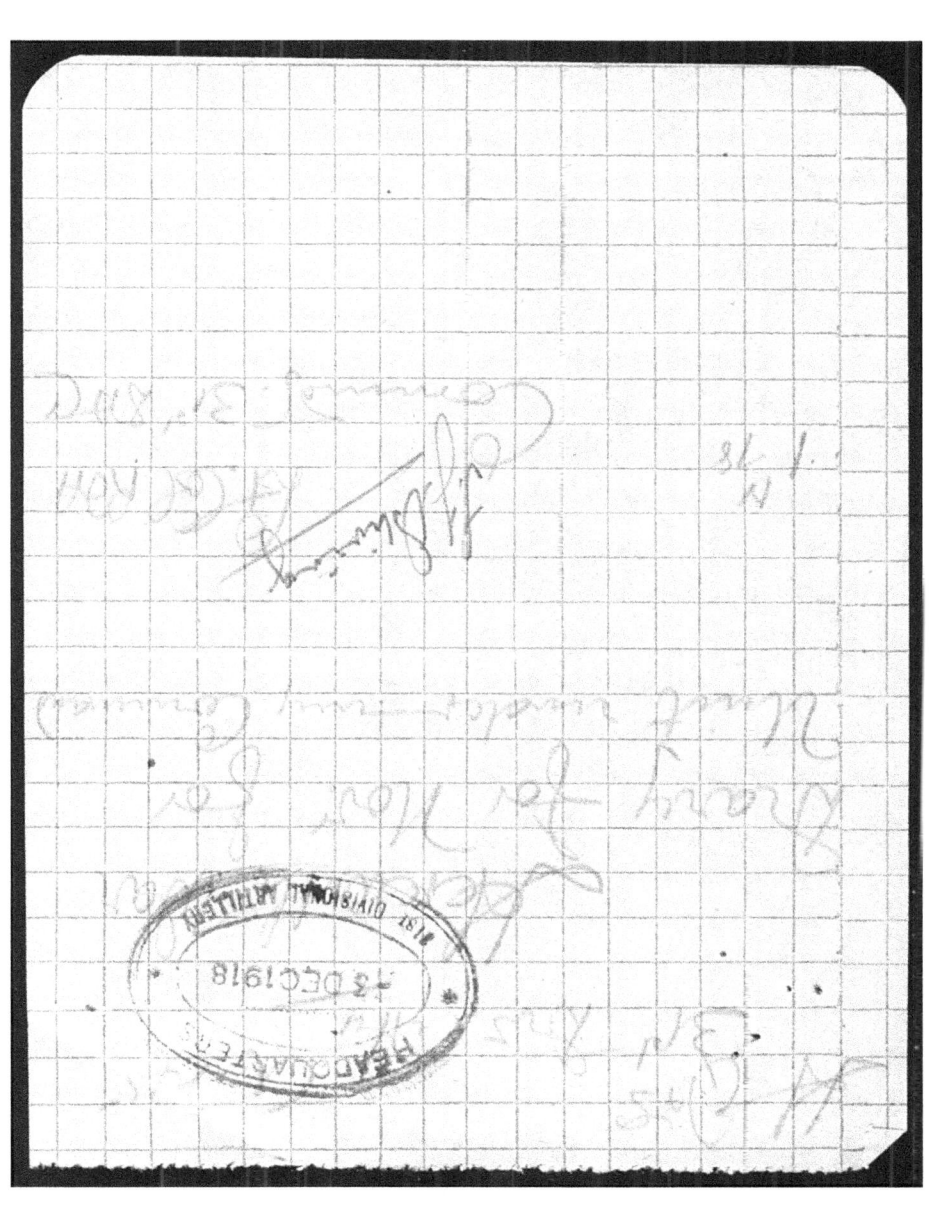

WAR DIARY

INTELLIGENCE SUMMARY

Army Form C. 2118.

3. BAC.

Nov 1918

Vol XXXV

Sheet 1

Place	Date	Hour	Summary of Events and Information	Remarks and references to Appendices
	1st		No 1 Sec. 16 G.25 Central (Sheet 29)	
	3rd		No 2 " 16 G.2 b 3.8 "	
			Hqrs " 16 O.35 Central (Sheet 28)	
	6th		No 1 " " "	
	7th		No 2 " " "	
			Hqrs " " O.35 b. 5.5.6	
			No 1 " " "	
			No 2 " " "	
			Hqrs " " M.13 a P.5"	
			No 1 " " M.14 c 2.3 (29 Sheet)	
			No 2 " " M.13 a 9.5	
			Hqrs " " O.5 c 3.9	
			No 1 " " O.5 c 0.9 (29 Sheet)	
			No 2 " " O.5 c 2.5	
	8th		Hqrs " " N.20 a 9.7 (29 Sheet)	
	10th		No 1 " " N.20 a 9.6	
			No 2 " " N.21 a 3.2	
	16th		Hqrs 1, 2, + Sections moved to Sweringhem	
	17th		do do Gullingham	

WAR DIARY or INTELLIGENCE SUMMARY

Army Form C. 2118.

3 DAC   Nov. 1918   Sheet 2

Place	Date	Hour	Summary of Events and Information	Remarks and references to Appendices
	26		Hdqrs No's 1, 2 & 3 DAA Secs move to Baron	
	27		do	Solesmes
	28		do	Avesnes
	29		do	Solre-le-Chateau
	30		do	Solrinnes

Signed J. Shinnie
Comdg 3e DAC Lt Col RFA

CONFIDENTIAL.

WAR DIARY

OF

31st DIVISIONAL AMMUNITION COLUMN.

From 1st December to 31st December, 1918.

VOLUME XXXVI.

WAR DIARY or INTELLIGENCE SUMMARY

Army Form C. 2118.

31st D.A.C. Vol XXVI

December 1918

Place	Date	Hour	Summary of Events and Information	Remarks and references to Appendices
Hellines	1st to 2nd		Divisional Mail	
Loqueires	7th to 9th		Column marches from Hellines to Laqueides	
" "	7th to 31st		Divisional detail - Auditing Horse Standings Demobilization & Education - Training Salvage Work	

J.B. Irving
Lieut Col RFA
Cmdg 31st DAC

CONFIDENTIAL.

WAR DIARY

OF

51st DIVISIONAL AMMUNITION COLUMN.

From 1st January to 31st January, 1919.

VOLUME XXXVII.

WAR DIARY or INTELLIGENCE SUMMARY

Army Form C. 2118.

Vol XXXVII 1 Feby 1919 — 31st February 1919

Place	Date	Hour	Summary of Events and Information	Remarks and references to Appendices
31 W.P.C	1/1/19 to 31/1/19		Salvage parties at work — demolished area. Demolition carting. Bees 14 2 or Companies + HQ.	

W. B. Ludgeon ?
Major 31 Div.

CONFIDENTIAL.

WAR DIARY

OF

31st DIVISIONAL AMMUNITION COLUMN.

From 1st February to 28th February, 1919.

VOLUME XXXVIII.

Vol XXVIII

WAR DIARY
or
INTELLIGENCE SUMMARY.

Army Form C. 2118

3/1 DAC Feb. 1919

Place	Date	Hour	Summary of Events and Information	Remarks and references to Appendices
Ezuodes	1st to 28th		HQ & No.s 1 & 2 Sections at Ezuodes	
St Quentin	1st to 28th		S.A.A. Sect. attached HQ. 66th Labour Group for salvage work in devastated area	

2879

J Faulkner Capt. RFA
9 Comdg 3/1 DAC

C O N F I D E N T I A L.

W A R   D I A R Y

O F

31st DIVISIONAL AMMUNITION COLUMN.

From 1st March to 31st March, 1919.

V O L U M E   XXXIX.

Original

31 2 D A C

Vol. XXIX

WAR DIARY
or
INTELLIGENCE SUMMARY.

(Erase heading not required.)

— March 1919.

Army Form C. 2118.

Place	Date	Hour	Summary of Events and Information	Remarks and references to Appendices
ESQUERDES	20		300 Lechan returned from Salvage Work at DICKIE BUSH.	

J Mitchell Lt A
Major
Comdg 31 DAC
2/4/19

CONFIDENTIAL

WAR DIARY

OF

31st DIVISIONAL AMMUNITION COLUMN.

From 1st April to 30th April, 1919.

VOLUME XL.

WAR DIARY
INTELLIGENCE SUMMARY

Army Form C. 218.

31st A.A.C. April 1919. No XL

Place	Date	Hour	Summary of Events and Information	Remarks and references to Appendices
Esquerdes	1st to 30th		Cadre Remains at Esquerdes	

) Nicholas Major RAA.
Comm'g. 31st A.A.C.